MY FIRST BOOK

MAURITIUS

ALL ABOUT MAURITIUS FOR KIDS

GLOBED
CHILDREN BOOKS

Interior and cover Design: Daniel Day
Editor: Margaret Bam

For My Sons, Daniel, David and Jude

Flic en Flac Beach, Mauritius

Mauritius

Mauritius is an island **country**.

A country is land that is controlled by a **single government**. Countries are also called **nations, states, or nation-states**.

Countries can be **different sizes**. Some countries are big and others are small.

Paradis Island, Blue Bay

Where Is Mauritius?

Mauritius is located in the continent of **Africa**.

A continent is **a massive area of land that is separated from others by water or other natural features**.

Mauritius is situated in the **Eastern part of Africa.**

Port Louis, Mauritius

Capital

The capital of Mauritius is Port Louis.

Port Louis is located in the **northwest coast** of the country.

Port Louis is the largest city in Mauritius.

Port Louis, Mauritius

Districts

Mauritius is divided into nine districts

The districts of Mauritius are

- **Port Louis District**
- **Pamplemousses District**
- **Rivière du Rempart District**
- **Flacq District**
- **Grand Port District**
- **Savanne District**
- **Plaines Wilhems District**
- **Moka District**
- **Black River District**

Population

Mauritius has a population of around **1.2 million people** making it the 48th most populated country in Africa and the 158th most populated country in the world.

Rochester Waterfalls, Mauritius

Size

Mauritius is **2,040 square kilometres** making it the 169th largest country in the world by area. Mauritius is the 52nd largest country in Africa.

Languages

Mauritius does not have an official language however English and French are generally considered to be de facto national languages.

The French-based creole language, Mauritian Creole is the lingua franca of the country and is widely spoken.

Here are a few phrases and sayings in Mauritian Creole

- **How are you? - Ki manyèr ?**
- **Good night - Bonswar**

Black River national park, Mauritius

Attractions

There are lots of interesting places to see in Mauritius.

Some beautiful places to visit in Mauritius are

- Port Louis Market
- Trou aux Biches Beach
- Pamplemousses Botanical Garden
- Chamarel Waterfall
- Black River Gorges National Park
- Le Morne Beach

Port Louis, Mauritius

History of Mauritius

Mauritius has a long and fascinating history. The area was first discovered by Arab sailors in the 10th century. In the 16th century, the island was claimed by the Dutch and named "Mauritius" after their ruler, Prince Maurice of Nassau.

In the 18th century, the French took over the island and made it a prosperous sugar colony. In the early 19th century, the British captured Mauritius from the French and ruled it for over 150 years. n 1968, Mauritius gained its independence from Britain and became a republic in 1992.

Pointe aux Canonniers, Mauritius

Customs in Mauritius

Mauritius has many fascinating customs and traditions.

- **Music and dance form an important part of Mauritian culture. Sega is a popular and traditional dance form of Mauritius. The dance is accompanied by drums, maracas and a triangle.**
- **Family is highly valued in Mauritian culture, and it is common for families to live together in extended households. Respect for elders is also an important value in Mauritian culture.**

Music of Mauritius

There are many different music genres in Mauritius such as **Sega, Bhojpuri, Reggae, and Indian Classical music.**

Some notable Mauritian musicians include
- **Cassiya**
- **Menwar**
- **Alain Ramanisum**
- **Linzy Bacbotte**
- **Eric Triton**

Food of Mauritius

Mauritian food is known for being tasty, delicious and flavoursome.

The national dish of Mauritius is Dholl puri which is a flatbread made from ground split peas (dhal) that is filled with cooked yellow split peas and served with a variety of condiments.

Traditional Mauritian food

Food of Mauritius

Mauritius cuisine is a fusion of African, Indian, Chinese, and European influences. Some popular dishes in Mauritius include

- Boulettes
- Gateau Piment
- Octopus Curry
- Fried Noodles
- Fish Vindaye
- Farata
- Rougaille
- Samosas

Baie du Cap, Mauritius

Weather in Mauritius

Mauritius has a **tropical climate**, which means that locals enjoy warm and sunny weather all year round.

There are two seasons in Mauritius: summer and winter. Summer is from November to April and is the rainy season, while winter is from May to October and is drier.

Mauritius cuckoo-shrike

Animals of Mauritius

There are many wonderful animals in Mauritius.

Here are some animals that live in Mauritius

- Pink pigeon
- Mauritian flying fox
- Telfair's skink
- Mauritius kestrel
- Mauritius parakeet
- Mauritius cuckoo-shrike

Trou aux Biches Beach

Beaches

There are many beautiful beaches in Mauritius which is one of the reasons why so many people visit this beautiful country every year.

Here are some of Mauritius' beaches

- Flic-en-Flac Beach
- Belle Mare Beach
- Grand Baie Beach
- Mont Choisy Beach
- Trou aux Biches Beach

Mauritius flag

Sports in Mauritius

Sports play an integral part in Mauritian culture. The most popular sport is Football.

Here are some of famous sportspeople from Mauritius

- Bruno Julie - Boxing
- Fabrice Bauluck - Swimming
- Kate Foo Kune - Badminton
- Jean-Marc Mormeck - Boxing
- Nafissatou Thiam - Heptathlon

Sir Seewoosagur Ramgoolam

Famous

Many successful people hail from Mauritius.

Here are some notable Mauritian figures

- **Ameenah Gurib-Fakim - President**
- **Ananda Devi - Writer**
- **Cédric Foo Kune - Footballer**
- **Joseph Reginald Topize - Prime Minister**
- **Lindsay Rivière - Musician**
- **Sir Seewoosagur Ramgoolam - Prime Minister**

The Morne Brabant, Mauritius

Something Extra...

As a little something extra, we are going to share some lesser known facts about Mauritius

- **Mauritius was once home to the now-extinct dodo bird.**
- **The national flag of Mauritius symbolizes the country's multi-ethnic and multicultural diversity.**

Chamarel Waterfall, Mauritius

Words From the Author

We hope that you enjoyed learning about the wonderful country of Mauritius.

Mauritius is a country rich in culture and beauty, with lots of wonderful places to visit and people to meet.

We hope you continue to learn more about this wonderful nation. If you enjoyed this book, consider leaving a review!

With Love

Printed in Great Britain
by Amazon

46996881R00027